Charleston: City of Memory

Along Queen Street.

Charleston:
CITY OF MEMORY

Photography by
N. Jane Iseley

Text by
Harlan Greene

LEGACY PUBLICATIONS
A Subsidiary of Pace Communications
Greensboro, North Carolina

The Pink House, Chalmers Street.

The pink house is perhaps the only house known for its color. It survives from the early Proprietary period of history. The street takes its name from Dr. Lionel Chalmers, the eighteenth-century physician famous for his work on fevers.

Copyright © 1987

Photography, N. Jane Iseley and Text, Harlan Greene

Book Design by Richard Stinely
Edited by D. J. Bost

Library of Congress Catalog Card Number:
87-81584 (Hardback Edition)
87-81585 (Softback Edition)

ISBN 0-933101-10-4 (Hardback Edition)
ISBN 0-933101-11-2 (Softback Edition)

Printed in Hong Kong by Everbest Printing Company
through Four Colour Imports Ltd., Louisville, Kentucky.

Every book on Charleston is a collaboration, drawing on the successes of others, not only those who have researched and written, but those who have protected, preserved and maintained. This book is dedicated to all who have contributed and who continue to contribute to the documentation and upkeep of the city.

**Col. William Rhett House,
54 Hasell Street.**

*Disguised by its later piazzas, the
Col. William Rhett House dates
from about 1712 and is the oldest
private house left in the city. The
builder captured the "gentleman
pirate" Stede Bonnet.*

They tell me she is beautiful, my City,
That she is colorful and quaint, alone
Among the cities. But I, I who have known
Her tenderness, her courage, and her pity,
Have felt her forces mould me, mind and bone,
Life after life, up from her first beginning.
How can I think of her in wood and stone!

SO wrote DuBose Heyward of Charleston, South Carolina, one of America's most beautiful and heroic cities. For over three hundred years now, those who have come here agree: There is something special about Charleston, something other than what can be seen. In her silences, in her streets, there is a wistfulness, a yearning, a poignancy. She dreams in her seasons, inducing a languor, as if from heat, so that she is impossible to forget and difficult to leave. She herself is compelled, almost narcissistically, to look from spire and dormer and balcony upon her sea-borne reflection, to ponder the deep significance of her history.

She was founded in 1670 as "Charles Towne," then the southernmost settlement in British North America. Departing Gravesend, England, her colonists were lured to this lush green Eden in search of a dream. Guided by the Cassique of Kiawah, a native Indian chief, the 150 or so colonists settled the west bank of the river they would call the Ashley.

Beginning a few years later, and completely by 1680, they moved to the present site of the city on the peninsula whose two rivers, the Cooper and the Ashley, flow together (so the local saying goes) to form the Atlantic Ocean. Each river takes its name from Anthony Ashley Cooper, Earl of Shaftesbury, one of the Lords Proprietors of the Colony. Although King Charles II gave his name to Carolina (through his Latin name Carolus) and to Charles Towne specifically, he gave the land itself to Shaftesbury and seven other gentlemen as a reward for their loyalty.

At the beginning of the eighteenth century, Charles Towne was a small walled city whose gates were at what is now the heart of downtown, the "four corners of law" at Broad and Meeting. Beyond them lay the luxurious semi-tropical forests as well as the enemy. The Spanish threatened periodically from St. Augustine; the Yemassee Indians, in their last uprising in 1715, burned the outlying settlements of the lowcountry and chased the refugees back to the very gates of the city. And in 1718, Captain William Rhett caught the pirate Stede Bonnet and brought him and his crew back to the city where they were hanged near the present-day Battery.

Buoyed by these early victories and feeling that

the Proprietors had not responded to their needs, these early Charlestonians displayed a burst of rebelliousness and self confidence that would soon become characteristic of the city. They rallied in assembly and relieved the Proprietors of Carolina, petitioning the Crown to become a Royal Colony.

By the time His Majesty's first royal governor arrived, Charles Towne was poised on her first spurt of growth – her walls were coming down and her streets continuing. There was a flurry of building all over, still evident today in a city noted for her visible history.

Styles for her mansions were imported and some came unchanged from England. Drayton Hall rose as a rural Palladian villa similar to many in the mother country and Miles Brewton built his correct Georgian house on King Street. Other forms, however, suffered a sea change, taking a touch from the French and influence from Barbados and the West Indies. The single house appeared as early as 1730, as singular in its name as in its narrowness and adaptability. You see them still on street after street, built in all eras and in all parts of the city. Some are on high arcaded basements, some on the ground, made of wood or brick; some are two stories, others, three. These houses are instantly recognizable: They have two rooms to a floor bisected by a stair hallway; windows across from each other pull a breeze under the high ceilings; and porches, never called anything but piazzas here, usually added to the

Miles Brewton House, 27 King Street.

With its tuscan and ionic columns of Portland stone, this is one of America's greatest Georgian Palladian mansions. Others have noticed the house's quality since its completion in 1769. Sir Henry Clinton and Lord Cornwallis commandeered it when Charleston fell in the Revolution, and Generals Meade and Hatch occupied it in the Civil War. It's said that the protective spikes over the fence date from the times of Denmark Vesey's failed slave rebellion.

south or west, keep sun from the windows and expand the living space significantly. Most of these piazzas have walls with doors separating them from the street so that opening a door in this city, you are often pleasantly confounded to find yourself still outside, or on a porch, at least. You have a garden to one side and the house with its main door to the other. By unspoken custom, should you have windows that face your neighbor's piazza, you do not look out of them, guaranteeing them their privacy, this being one of the elegant compromises that make life so pleasant in this densely populated but polite city. What is striking about the single house is its orientation: It sits sideways, narrow or gable end to the street; and so it is symbolic of both the city and her inhabitants. From one angle, Charlestonians and their city may appear too aloof and proud and forbidding to approach; but looked at from a less formal and more intimate angle, they, like their houses, are open and friendly. Stretching out behind the single houses, back into the deep narrow lots, are all the outbuildings, each additional one smaller than the last, looking like a nest of Chinese boxes – the kitchen, slave quarters, stables and other dependencies.

The other style of house that developed here as early is the double house, a name that should give rise to no double meanings or misunderstandings, which are often quite unavoidable here where Legare is pronounced Legree; Porcher, Porshay; and Huger, Hugee. A double house, of course, has twice as many rooms to a floor – there are four, often two

9

61, 69 and 71 Church Street.

These buildings, taken together, offer a concise architectural history. The First Baptist Church, founded in 1682, commissioned Robert Mills to design their building, whose ca. 1820 Greek Revival portico is seen here. Next to it is an early and large double house; it was the home of Alice Ravenel Huger Smith, a watercolorist of supreme delicacy, who is often acknowledged as being the first to paint her house one of the pastel colors now prevalent here. The narrow house with the balcony was built by Robert Brewton about 1730. A National Historic Landmark, it is the prototype of the single house and the earliest one surviving.

The Robert Brewton House, 71 Church Street.

Growing narrower, the successive stages of the house retreat towards the garden, which was designed by Loutrell Briggs, author of **Charleston Gardens.**

Boone Hall Plantation, Slave Street.

*These brick and tile cabins, built in 1843, were used
by the house servants of the Horlbeck family, who
ran a brickyard here as well, supplying the city.
Boone Hall, across the Cooper River, is open to
the public.*

A Street Garden.

*One of the flower ladies, displaying her blossoms
near the corner of Broad and Meeting. You can buy
a Gullah basket as well, the product of a surviving
folk art brought over from Africa in the late seven-
teenth century. Often made of black rush, palmetto
and sweetgrass, with tools ranging from needles to
nails to spoon handles, these baskets are made in
several shapes and sizes. The term Gullah also
refers to the language that resulted from English
words being grafted onto African syntax. You can
still hear it in the streets and on the sea islands.*

The Huguenot Church, 136 Church Street.

This gothic gem was built in 1844 to the designs of Edward Brickell White to replace an earlier church. It is the only independent French Calvinist congregation in the country. The pinnacles are capped with cast-iron; the organ inside is the original, by Henry Ebern.

on either side of a central hall. On an upper level, a larger room, such as a ballroom or drawing room for entertaining, may stretch across the whole front. Both single and double houses are often graced with wrought-iron balconies.

Sometimes there are clues: initials in iron or brick, or dates in chimneys or at doorways. But for the most part, we do not know the names of the architects or cabinetmakers who executed the ornate carvings, just as we do not know the names of the slaves who provided the labor and often made the bricks on outlying plantations. We do know, however, that it was rice, introduced to Carolina quite early, that made the mansions and plantations possible and slavery necessary. By 1708, so many African slaves had been brought into Charles Towne and the surrounding lowcountry that they had already achieved a black majority. The delicate interplay of black and white that would write Charleston's history began quite early. Their overlapping chronicles are as connected and fretted as the coils in the sweetgrass Gullah baskets sold in the city Market.

While rice was pouring its gold into the city, another hue deepened her prosperity: Indigo, the berry that produced the rich purplish-blue dye so prized in the eighteenth century, was introduced and first grown successfully by the fifteen-year-old Eliza Lucas. For this, England paid a handsome bounty.

With these crops and trade with England, Charles Towne grew to be the wealthiest and fourth largest city in the colonies. She was as sophisticated in her

11

Beth Elohim Synagogue and St. Mary's Roman Catholic Church, Hasell Street.

Although there were Jews here in the 1690's, they did not form a congregation until 1749. It was orthodox Sephardic. A split occurred in 1824 with the founding of the Reformed Society of Israelites, which launched the reform movement in this country. It was in this building, built in 1840, that the first organ was installed in a Jewish house of worship in America. Founded in 1789, St. Mary's is the Mother Church for Catholics in Georgia and the Carolinas. The first to celebrate mass were the Irish; French Catholics arrived soon after from Santo Domingo. Both congregations, when faced with replacing buildings destroyed in an 1838 fire, chose designs inspired by Greek and Roman temples.

12

tastes as she was diverse in her inhabitants. Huguenots, or French protestants, had arrived in the city about 1680. Spanish Jews came next, in the 1690's, establishing and subsequently building what is now the oldest synagogue in continual use in this country. (Quite fittingly, the church of the first Catholic parish in the Carolinas and Georgia is just across the street.) Charles Towne also attracted Baptists, Quakers and Methodists, as well as many other denominations.

But Charleston was more of a secular, even a sensual, city. There was opera (in 1735 – the first one recorded in this country), and dance and drama,

Hibernian Hall, 105 Meeting Street.

This Irish Benevolent Society was founded in 1801 and built its hall in 1840. Elected annually, its presidents alternate between Protestant and Catholic. The St. Cecilia balls and other social functions are held here. The anachronistic window in the pediment dates from after 1886, when the earthquake sent the whole portico toppling.

Dock Street Theatre, Corner of Church and Queen.

Once called Dock Street, it was near here on Queen Street that Charleston's first theatre opened in 1737. The building had disappeared by 1809 when the Planters Hotel began operating. The central portion, with its indented entry, brownstone columns and airy balcony, was added later when the hotel was one of the most sumptuous in the South, housing the actor Junius Brutus Booth during his stay in the city. He would, no doubt, be pleased to know its subsequent history. In danger of demolition, the building was saved and reconstructed in 1935 as an eighteenth century theatre by the WPA. Many events of the Spoleto Arts Festival are held here.

Daniel Elliot Huger House, 34 Meeting Street.

The calm facade of the Daniel Elliot Huger house belies its exciting history. Lord William Campbell, the last royal governor, fled it under the cover of night and Lafayette was later entertained here. It was damaged in the siege of 1863 - 1865 and looted by Federal troops. Yet it maintains its serenity.

including outstanding seasons of Shakespeare. Gentlemen banded together to found a private library in 1743, still surviving; the museum founded in Charles Towne now functions as the oldest in the country. And the St. Cecilia Society, instituted as a musical club, still hosts balls open only to elite society.

Charlestonians developed early into a studious and eternally curious breed, interested in all aspects of science and natural history. The gardenia takes its name from John Garden of this city; and the perennially popular Christmas flower, the poinsettia, would come to be christened after Charleston's diplomat, Joel Roberts Poinsett. Audubon would be a frequent visitor here, too; but perhaps even more

telling than this is the fact that William Charles Wells was born here. Wells, after leaving Charleston in the Revolution, prefigured Charles Darwin in formulating the theory of natural selection.

By the 1760's, however, political developments held center stage in the city. The Stamp Act and other import duties angered and frustrated Charlestown, as she was now being called; more than any other colonial city, she was more closely linked by ties of trade and family to the mother country. But the old spirit of independence and self-confidence that had overthrown the Proprietors in 1719 was again surfacing. The last royal governor had to flee under the cover of night before the colony declared her independence on March 26, 1776. Just a

**Broad Street and the
Exchange Building.**

This street, as one novelist would have it, is the "boundary between longing and belonging." Not only is it Charleston's Wall Street, it runs from river to river, separating the parishes of St. Michael's and St. Philip's, and acts as the line of demarcation to "South of Broad," the prime residential section. At its foot is the Exchange Building. Since its construction in 1771, it has witnessed much history: The beginning of state government; the imprisonment of patriots in the Revolution; the ratification of the Constitution and George Washington's visit. It has served as a customs house, the post office, city hall, and offices for the Light House Department. Owned by the D.A.R., it is run by a commission that keeps part of the building open to the public.

St. Michael's Steeple from Church Street.

Having served as a colonial lighthouse, an observation tower in the Revolution, a signal post in the Civil War, and as an air raid siren station in World War II, St. Michael's has earned the right to keep a proprietary watch over the city. Her bells are "far less like bells than chanted memories."

St. Michael's Episcopal Church, 80 Meeting Street.

St. Michael's Episcopal Church is the oldest church building in the city, being finished in 1761. Distinguished worshippers included George Washington and Robert E. Lee. Two signers of the Constitution lie in her cemetery. St. Michael's stands at the intersection of Broad and Meeting, the "four corners of law": God's law is represented by the church, Federal law by the U.S. Court and Post Office, County law is represented by the county courthouse, Municipal jurisdiction by City Hall.

St. Michael's Alley.

The stuccoed building with the balcony was the law office of James Louis Petigru, Charleston's staunch Unionist. An opponent of Calhoun, he was nevertheless respected for his firm beliefs and honored by his city. St. Michael's steeple keeps a watch over its namesake alley.

16

76 and 78 Church Street.

These two houses have been combined into one dwelling. The small house to the right was where DuBose Heyward read of the real-life Sammy Smalls and conceived the original idea for Porgy. It's said that George Washington addressed the city from an earlier balcony on the other building. Note the circular earthquake bolts, the most common type in the city.

short time later, on June 28, Carolina turned back the British fleet just beyond the city at the battle of Fort Moultrie. Bells still ring in town on that day to commemorate Carolina Day; and the palmetto, of which the fort was made, and which is seen on Charleston's streets, is now the state tree.

Charlestown remained relatively free of the enemy until 1780. Then she was besieged and suffered much in the bombardment. It was even rumored that the 1778 fire that had destroyed much of the early city had been set by the British. The city was surrendered and occupied in May of 1780. Many of her citizens were arrested and carried off in a prison ship to St. Augustine. Colonel Isaac Hayne was taken from the prisons beneath the Exchange Building and hanged outside the city.

The town and her people suffered many more indignities. When the British retreated in 1782, they took what they could, looting much of the disposable wealth of the city. Even the church bells were taken from St. Michael's steeple, although they were returned by a London merchant. After the treaty of peace was signed in 1783, Charleston was incorporated, and she took that name officially.

Plants grow lushly in the lowcountry's subtropical atmosphere and wounds heal quickly. By 1791, when President George Washington visited and climbed St. Michael's steeple, he could look out and see a city well on her way to what must have seemed her permanent rendezvous with prosperity. Her streets were continuing southward to what is now White Point Garden and the Battery; her wharves were thronged to the east; to the north, she grew past what is now the Market and surrounded

The Heyward-Washington House, 87 Church Street.

This house takes its hyphenated name from Daniel Heyward, who built the three-story brick mansion, and from George Washington, who stayed here during his 1791 visit. Heyward's son Thomas signed the Declaration of Independence, and his later descendant DuBose referred to the house in Porgy. But with the vagaries of time, the house became a slum and the bottom floor was turned into a bakery. The house was saved in a group preservation movement in the late 1920's. It is now owned by the Charleston Museum, which opens the house to the public.

18

Heyward-Washington House, Drawing Room.

The fully paneled room features an elaborately carved overmantel and a tea table, both attributed to the Charleston master, Thomas Elfe. The Chippendale chairs once graced Drayton Hall. The window in the stair hall looks out to the garden and a full array of outbuildings.

Ansonborough, once a suburb well outside the limits. And to the west, Harleston Village, a fashionable new part of town, was developing. There was new building going on in all parts of the city.

Nathaniel Russell, who had been loyal to England but who joined his fate to the city's, built his elegant geometric mansion on Meeting Street. Gabriel Manigault, from one of the wealthiest families in town,

Nathaniel Russell House, Staircase.

Although he put his initials in iron on his front balcony, the free-flying staircase, rising three floors, may serve as Nathaniel Russell's most famous "signature." It is justly the most famous staircase in the city.

Nathaniel Russell House, 51 Meeting Street.

Called "King of the Yankees" – no doubt with some envy – Nathaniel Russell finished his elegant mansion by 1809. Of special note are its oval rooms and encircling balconies. Gov. R.F.W. Allston was a later owner of the house and his daughter kept a school here after the Civil War, as did the Sisters of Our Lady of Mercy. The Historic Charleston Foundation maintains it as a house museum.

20

designed and built a bank (now city hall), a home for his brother Joseph, and a home for the South Carolina Society. William Blacklock raised his imposing mansion on Bull Street; all these structures built in the Federal period are still standing. The flurry of activity, however, was cut short by the War of 1812. Two steepleless churches still bear witness to the deep economic depression that hit the city.

Recovery was slow this time; the 1820's and 30's were a time of decline. The country was growing away from Charleston, growing to the north and west, shifting away from her plantation base to industry. To catch up with the developments, the city reached; she set out the longest railroad in the world, all of one hundred and thirty miles away to Hamburg, to the west; and the Santee Canal system was her ambitious attempt to link her interior to the sea. But nonetheless, her status as a port and as a metropolis was slipping. The South, however, if not the country as a whole, still saw Charleston as an arbiter of taste and seat of power. If cotton was being crowned king, then Charleston would rise as cotton's queen city. And cotton, like rice before it, demanded slavery.

Timothy Ford House, 54 Meeting Street.

Seen from the Russell House garden across the street, this house is graced with handsome Adam interiors and a fragrant cascade of wisteria all along its fence. It was the home of Edmund Ravenel, a distinguished nineteenth-century naturalist.

William Blacklock House, 18 Bull Street.

The brickwork and windows in arches, accented with stone, as well as the delicate side and fan lights of the front door, make William Blacklock's ca. 1800 house one of the most noteworthy in town. It is owned by the College of Charleston Foundation.

21

Joseph Manigault House, 350 Meeting Street.

Gabriel Manigault designed this house, built in 1801, for his brother Joseph. In 1920, when it was threatened with destruction, a group of Charlestonians organized to save it, launching the preservation movement. The dwelling was saved, but a gas station (since removed) was built in the garden. Entered from the gate house, it is kept open by the Charleston Museum.

South Carolina Society Hall, 72 Meeting Street.

It was Charleston's "gentleman architect," Gabriel Manigault, who designed this 1804 building. In 1825, Frederick Wesner added the portico. The organization was founded in 1737 as a benevolent society. The view from the garden across the street shows the difference between private piazza and public portico.

22

Manigault House, Ballroom

Elizabeth Wragg Manigault, in her portrait by Jeremiah Theus, looks out on the ballroom of the Manigault house built by one of her sons for another. The vases on the mantel are French, the furniture English Regency. The carpet is Aubusson and the tea table was made in Charleston. Folding panels under the window make it a door leading to the piazza.

143 Tradd Street.

*Rumor has it that this cast- and wrought-iron gate,
with its rare arrow design, was to be used by the
hapless followers of the slave rebellion leader
Denmark Vesey. The house, once on the marshes
of the Ashley River, looks mysterious down its
long walkway.*

This ownership of human souls was always the dark underbelly of the city's history. Scattered outbreaks of violence and rebellion had occurred since the founding. And in June of 1822, the free man of color Denmark Vesey (who had bought his freedom with money won in a lottery) was arrested for planning a revolt that was supposed to have brought as many as six thousand slaves rushing in from the country. The loyal slave who informed on him was given his freedom, but, ironically, new laws were enacted making it nearly impossible for a slave to be freed. This strict treatment of slaves so angered Sarah and Angelina Grimké that they left Charleston forever and became leaders in the abolitionist and women's rights movement. (Another set of Charleston sisters, the Pollitzers, would take up their cudgels, becoming leaders in the women's movement and the National Women's Party in the twentieth century.)

Adrift from the industrialist and abolitionist interests of the country, Charleston turned her vision inward. Her native son, the architect Robert Mills, adorned Charleston with a variety of distinguished and innovative buildings – the Marine Hospital, the First Baptist Church and the Fireproof Building, now the home of the South Carolina Historical Society. Many buildings, lacking this fireproof construction, were destroyed in the Great Fire of 1838. Whole neighborhoods were built back, often in the sumptuous style of the day – Greek revival. Charlestonians have never been an ostentatious breed; if they added grand porticoes to their houses, they often did not put them on the front, but tucked

them discreetly to the side, where the piazzas would be. They saved the Greek and Roman temple style for their public buildings – Market Hall, Hibernian Hall and numerous churches throughout town. Porticoes were added to the College of Charleston and South Carolina Society Hall. The effect must have been grand, but at the same time, eerie; for in the

Fireproof Building, 100 Meeting Street.

Begun in 1822, it took five years for this Charleston District Records Office to be finished. Robert Mills, its architect, used brick floors, walls and ceilings, and metal windows and roof to protect its contents from fire. The building is still carrying out its mission, now housing the South Carolina Historical Society, founded in 1855 to document the state's history. Washington Park surrounds the building on two sides and it faces a street corner, isolating it further from the hazards of fire. The gate is ca. 1858 by C. Werner.

The Marine Hospital, 20 Franklin Street.

This Robert Mills structure is the city's first gothic revival building, built at Federal expense in 1834. Originally intended for ailing merchant seamen, it went on to be used as a teaching hospital for the Medical College of South Carolina, and a hospital for the Confederacy. From 1891 - 1939, the Reverend Daniel Jenkins ran an orphanage here for black children. He started a band, sending it up and down the streets, playing for money; it went on to tour Europe and to appear in the Broadway version of Porgy. So many jazz greats came out of Jenkins' orphanage that one recent historian has called it a "Jazz Nursery."

College of Charleston, 66 George Street.

If truth is beauty and beauty truth, you can do no better than to attend the College of Charleston. Founded in 1785, it was the first municipal college in the country; it is now part of the state system. Randolph Hall was built in 1826 and had a portico added in 1850. The college endeavors to provide a classical education in a classic setting.

11 College Street.

This rounded and turreted Queen Anne mansion was built in 1891 by Samuel Wilson. It is now surrounded by a pedestrian mall on the College campus and is used as a dormitory.

27

twilight of the antebellum era, the city was beginning to resemble the Greek City State, whose role she was fulfilling. She would, with her fall, lead the Carolina lowcountry and the whole South on to doom, like a heroine in Greek tragedy.

Charleston was unwilling, even unable, to give up slavery, the source of her prosperity. John C. Calhoun, with his doctrine of state's rights, epitomized her political beliefs. He had been born upstate, but she claimed him for her own, for Eternity. When he died in 1850, Charleston was draped in black, his body lay in state, and he was buried in St. Philip's cemetery.

With Abraham Lincoln's election as president, the old Charleston spirit was stirring. A convention was held in St. Andrew's Hall (since burned), and on December 20, 1861, South Carolina seceded from the Union and became the nucleus of the Southern Confederacy.

Market Hall, 188 Meeting Street.

There's been a city market here since the 1780's and probably always will be. If not, the land will revert back to the Pinckney family which donated it to the city. Market Hall, with bull and ram heads in its frieze (the meat market was here), houses a Confederate Museum, and "sheds" stretch out behind it with vegetables, souvenirs and boutiques. Nightclubs, restaurants and streetlife abound along Market Street

St. Philip's Episcopal Church, 146 Church Street.

Dominating not just the skyline, St. Philip's Episcopal Church has also played a great role in the city's history. Joseph Hyde designed the present building which replaced an earlier structure that burned in 1835. The steeple was added in 1850. John C. Calhoun, DuBose Heyward and Edward Rutledge, signer of the Declaration of Independence, are buried in the cemetery.

St. Philip's Cemetery.

Philip's Church.

e light-filled interior contrasts atly with its earth-colored exterior. e memorial sculpture of grief is in mory of William Mason Smith, a tryman who guided the rebuilding.

Marion Square, Calhoun Street.

With an enigmatic expression on his face and his bronze cape unfurling behind him, John C. Calhoun surveys the city. As secretary of war, Vice President and member of Congress, Calhoun was a force in national politics until his death in 1850. Some 40 years later, the city placed his likeness on a literal pedestal that he had been occupying metaphorically. Behind him is the old Citadel, built as the arsenal after the 1822 slave rebellion. In 1843, it became the home of the South Carolina Military Academy, also known as the Citadel, which moved to a larger campus in 1922.

30

She also was the battle queen. On April 12, 1861, at about 4:00 in the morning, people rushed to their rooftops and to the railings along High Battery to see history in the making. The Civil War had just begun with the shelling of the Union-held Fort Sumter in the center of the harbor. Had they known what it would mean for their city and their country, no doubt the people in the streets would not have cheered so fiercely that morning.

All southern ports were blockaded almost immediately, and by 1863, the city was under siege; shells fell and did great damage throughout the town; the populace withdrew from their range to above Calhoun Street. A great fire had burned from river to river in 1861, destroying one-third of the city, adding to the scene of desolation. To the soldier holding watch up in St. Michael's steeple, scanning the harbor for the movements of the enemy, the city must have looked as ruined as Pompeii. Grass grew up in the streets; windows and doors stood open; the houses were looted and empty. A city once praised for its Asiatic splendor now seemed utterly doomed.

And there seemed no doubt of it after Savannah fell in 1864, and word was received that Sherman was coming. The official correspondence foretold Charleston's destruction — she would be razed and have her soil sown with salt, like a city in biblical prophecy. Nearly all her valuables, including the

Fort Sumter from the Battery.

It's quite a spot for musing. Here the lower walk rises and becomes "High Battery"; beyond the seawall, the Ashley and Cooper rivers meet. Ft. Sumter can be clearly seen. All eyes were on it on April 12, 1861, when the Confederates on James Island (the land mass on the right) began firing on the Union-held Fort Sumter, starting the Civil War. Major Robert Anderson surrendered 34 hours later.

101 - 107 Bull Street.

Unusual in Charleston, the row house is more typical of her sister city to the south, Savannah. This harmonious group was built in the early 1850's, and in the Civil War, blockade-run merchandise was offered for sale here.

bells of St. Michael's, were sent to Columbia, the state capital, for safekeeping. But Sherman veered. On February 17, the day Charleston was evacuated, Columbia was burned to the ground.

Charleston was silent for years. The surviving St. Michael's bells were recast and returned to the city, but they tolled only in memory. A Manigault worked in the poorhouse; a Middleton rented rooms. And DuBose Heyward's father, Ned, descendant of the signer of the Declaration of Independence, whose father's house had been used to entertain George Washington on his visit, barely eked out a living as a hand in a rice mill.

"Too poor to paint and too proud to whitewash," Charlestonians held on to their heritage. For them, their physical city was, and still is, tangible proof – the repository – of their history. Traditional single houses adapted to the late nineteenth century were built on side lots and gardens sold off from earlier mansions. Although some Victorian houses were built, and some were remodeled in the contemporary style, for the most part, people followed the old ways, remaining true to their city. But it would be a mistake to say that this was a new belief or that it was all a matter of economic necessity. At Drayton Hall, for instance, the Drayton family had made no major changes since the house was begun in the 1730's. The same sort of time-capsule quality reigned over the whole city. Later, in the twentieth century, another Charleston family would call in photographers to record their parlors; then they turned the key, sealing the rooms for over half a century.

Drayton Hall.

It must have looked very similar to this that day in 1865 when Federal troops raided the plantations along the Ashley River. Although most were destroyed, Drayton Hall was saved; no one knows why. Perhaps its other-worldliness, its surviving from an earlier time, kept it from the contemporary fray. Barely changed since its completion in 1742, the house, with no electricity or plumbing, is owned by the National Trust and open to the public.

Calhoun Mansion, 16 Meeting Street.

With over a score of rooms, three floors, endless piazzas and an attic, this is one of the largest houses in town. Built by the merchant prince George Walton Williams in 1876, it disproves two things: Everyone was poor after the Civil War; and there is no Victorian architecture of note in Charleston. A house museum.

There were storms that destroyed her crops and drove ships into her streets. She suffered silently. And then Time stopped for her when, on August 31, 1886, at 9:51 on a hot summer evening, St. Michael's bells pealed. The clock hands stopped as an earthquake rocked the city, sinking steeples, toppling porticoes and chimneys, killing, injuring, damaging nearly every building in the entire city. Earthquake bolts and rods were run through to strengthen the old walls, and stucco, used to cover the repairs in the brick, became more popular.

It was her tragic past and gentle beauty that began to bring the curious here. "Pathos adheres to this very earth," wrote one visitor at the time. Arriving at the turn of the century to stay for a few weeks, the writer John Bennett lingered for more than half a century.

But Time was slowly waking this Sleeping Beauty. There was an economic revival brought about by the phosphate industry; an interstate trade fair was held on the old racecourse grounds outside town. Mostly, however, it was World War I that brought Charleston into the modern era. It did not bring its desolation and destruction here; instead it brought money, visitors and sailors from the navy yard into the streets. With Europe closed to the rich, and the Florida land boom beginning, many travellers stopped in to see the forgotten, ancient-looking city. Charleston was quaint and appealing. People ate dinner at 3:00, creating a sort of siesta in the shops and banks and law firms on Broad Street. Vegetable vendors, with their wares on their heads, called out in a strange patois as they hawked them

Calhoun Mansion, Dining Room.

The dining room of the Calhoun Mansion has stenciled walls, and golden oak paneling. Under the brass and nickel chandelier, whose globes are etched with rice planting scenes, a rosewood table and its original leather chairs seat ten — comfortably. The paintings over the buffet are by the local painter Thomas Wightman.

on the streets. Shuttered houses with delicate wrought-iron balconies looked towards their gardens, from above whose high walls the smell of wisteria and tea olive rose and fell like sighs over the city. There was a mellowness in the air; to Henry James, visiting in 1902, the forts, faintly blue on the horizon, seemed to hover on the harbor like water lilies. In the evenings, with church bells ringing, lilac-colored bricks gave off stored heat, and the whole city seemed to breathe of other times, other memories.

The wealthy who came bought up deserted plantations and hunted ducks in the old rice reserves; writers and artists wintered here. And Sinclair Lewis, author of *Main Street*, had his fictional character Carol Kennicott come to Charleston to recover from the madness of the materialistic culture of the twentieth century. Charleston, with her dignity and her beauty, offered a balm to these refugees.

But visitors were taking away more than mere memories; they were taking souvenirs – a balcony here, a doorway there; sometimes entire rooms and whole houses were dismantled and shipped away

Villa Margherita, 4 South Battery.

"It was in the Villa Margherita by the palms of the Charleston Battery ... that her aloofness melted." So Sinclair Lewis wrote of Carol Kennicott in his novel Main Street. She joins the ranks of the famous who have stayed here. It was built in 1892 for Daisy Simonds who persuaded President Theodore Roosevelt to dine here during his 1902 visit. In 1909, it became a guest house, later accommodating Gertrude Stein and other notables and literati. The house to the left was built by Col. William Washington, George Washington's kinsman.

36

A Rooftop View.

Steeples (of the First Scots Presbyterian Church, ca. 1814), gables, dormers, and trees. Height ordinances for new structures now protect the skyline of the city.

**Aiken-Rhett House,
48 Elizabeth Street.**

*Starting in 1817 as a single house,
this house grew over the years.
Gov. William Aiken remodeled it
in the Italianate style and built an
art gallery for his superb
collection. The interior stair hall
is marble. Both can be seen since
the Rhett family gave the house to
the Charleston Museum, which
keeps it open.*

Aiken-Rhett House, Parlors.

Governor Aiken bought the chandeliers from a nobleman's estate sale in Paris in 1833 to hang in these double parlors, which are graced with a life-size portrait of his wife. Jefferson Davis was entertained in these rooms and, in 1864, General Beauregard was headquartered here. The rooms were sealed in 1918 and not opened until 1972. Restoration is ongoing.

for reassembling. Others took with them the dance step of the Charleston that they had seen black children practice in the street for a shower of tossed pennies. And so, ironically, the slow, regal city gave her name to the dance that seemed to epitomize the wild new century. It was advancing down her streets with a ravening need, tearing down old buildings; parking lots appeared. A "skyscraper" rose on Broad Street; a gas station sprouted in the garden of the Joseph Manigault house. It seemed that time itself, in the guise of progress, was the enemy. Surely, it would destroy the city.

But Charlestonians have always stood up for their beliefs, and they believe most strongly in their city. It is more than mortar holding the old walls together; it is memory. Private citizens bought condemned old houses and saved them from destruction. They banded together to found the Society for the Preservation of Old Dwellings. In 1931, the city passed the first zoning laws in the country. To save herself, the city began saving her history, protecting her old buildings just as if they were an endangered species. But they were not to become extinct like the Carolina Paroquet that Audubon had drawn, and which had flourished here in great numbers before disappearing. Over the years, the Old and Historic District, and the laws protecting it, have grown proportionally. The motto of the city adopted in 1783, and translated as "she protects her customs, buildings and her laws," has proved to be one of prophecy.

73 King Street.

This handsome house at the corner of King and Tradd Streets features unstuccoed brick, lacy ironwork and trim painted "Charleston green." Bamboo grows in the gateway.

36 and 38 Chalmers Street.

These two handsome houses are linked to women important in the cultural life of the city. The unstuccoed brick house was the birthplace of etcher Elizabeth O'Neill Verner and later the residence of Laura Mary Bragg, director of the Charleston Museum, and center of the last salon in the city. The house to the right belonged to her good friend Josephine Pinckney who wrote movingly and affectionately of Charleston. Built by free woman of color Jane Wightman, both were modernized by the preservation architect, Albert Simons.

41

Cabbage Row, 89-91 Church Street.

Alias "Catfish Row," this is often the first building visitors ask to see. For it was here, next to the house of his ancestor, that DuBose Heyward set his novel Porgy, changing its name slightly in the process and moving it closer to the water. It is a typical double tenement with an alley to its rear courtyard in the center. The whole neighborhood became a slum; scores of people were living here by the 20th century. Porgy was published in 1925; in 1927, with the help of Heyward's wife Dorothy, it was a Broadway play; in 1935, it became an opera with music by George Gershwin. The ground floor contains two shops — Porgy and, you guessed it, Bess.

It was this era, as well, that gave birth to Charleston's most famous citizen, DuBose Heyward's Porgy, that fictional black beggar based on a real character who once roamed Charleston's streets. It is not ironic but fitting that this noble black man, created by a scion of white aristocracy, has taken Charleston's story to the world. The opera *Porgy and Bess* has gone to London, Moscow, Rome and Vienna – indeed to all cultures on all continents. And the tale of Porgy – his triumph and despair, his belief in his dreams – is really the story of the city.

Today Charleston is not so much a city that lives in her past as one that allows it to live in her streets. All of her epochs, her incarnations as Charles Towne, Charlestown, and Charleston, exist simultaneously. Horse carriages compete with trucks; jets streak past eighteenth-century steeples; young children bear old names heavy with history; and rock music ricochets down cobbled alleys. There are often tiny epiphanies. When, on a recent New Year's Eve, there was a power failure, candles were lit, gas came coursing through the old jets, and those out in the flame-lit street could see what Charleston had looked like in an earlier century: She reached into her past to sustain herself while moving inexorably on into another year. The city's "secret" was guessed by artist Elizabeth O'Neill Verner, who realized that Charleston and Time have made peace. Charleston takes the best of past and present and looks to the future calmly.

All who live here today look upon the city with understandable pride. For Charlestonians take their rice with butter, their scotch neat and their history

Colonial Lake.

Settled first on the Cooper River, the city eventually reached the Ashley as its western boundary. It wasn't until 1881 that city council developed this old millpond near the Ashley River. The two single houses have looked upon sunsets for more than a century.

43

209-235 Meeting Street.

The buildings in this row date from 1840 to 1914, incorporating a variety of styles with common cast-iron store fronts. They were the scene of a major preservation battle that required the wisdom of Solomon to settle. Now part of a hotel and shopping complex, the rear of the buildings were torn down for a parking garage while the front halves were saved for boutiques and businesses.

very personally. It's only natural that, living in the same rooms, walking the same streets, they feel a personal kinship with their ancestors and the earlier eras of the city. Portraits have an odd, *dejá vu*-like quality and time plays a fugue here, repeating old themes differently.

Although they may not take their main meal at 3:00, Charleston residents still eat rice and she crab soup and hoppin' john on New Year's. They sit on piazzas and paint their shutters "Charleston green." They dislike difference and encourage eccentricity. They go to oyster roasts at Rockville and to St. Cecilia balls where the guest list is determined by inheritance and geography. They live in a city that demands good manners yet smiles tolerantly on many things, as anyone must who has seen for so long the vanity and nobility of the human species. She just may be that combination of Mediterranean manners and Caribbean ways suggested by John Bennett. And although her children have evolved into a wandering breed, even giving the word maverick to the English language (before they started wandering, the Mavericks were a Charleston family), they nevertheless are loyal. Like pilgrims to Mecca, they always return; and it is for the veneration in which she is held, by visitor and resident alike, and not in tribute to her religious history, that Charleston is often affectionately called "The Holy City."

The poet DuBose Heyward put it most succinctly. He wrote:

> *Hers are the eyes through which I look on life*
> *And find it brave and splendid. And the stir*
> *Of hidden music shaping all my songs,*
> *And these my songs, my all, belong to her.*

Devotion such as this from all her people in all her centuries has protected her heritage, preserved her ways, and made Charleston one of America's most distinctive and distinguished cities.

Patriot's Point.

The Yorktown, *seen here, is just one of the ships in the Maritime Museum that grew out of the local Bicentennial commemoration. Charleston Harbor, with its centuries of naval history, is a perfect setting. The local public radio station is housed on the* Yorktown.

City of Memory

**St. Philip's Gates,
Western Cemetery.**

*This wrought-iron gate is one
of the oldest and most delicate
in the city.*

Edmonston-Alston House, Drawing Room.

This room, one of two, with matching green glass English chandeliers, contains a ca. 1848 Ridgeway tea service of the Alston family, an 1811 harp by Sebastian Erard and a rosewood pianoforte inlaid with mahogany, satinwood and brass mountings. The window behind the Sheraton settee opens onto the balcony; the door, to the library.

**Edmonston-Alston House,
21 East Battery.**

*This house was built by Charles
Edmonston in 1828; he was forced
to sell it a decade later in losses
from a financial panic. Charles
Alston bought it and added the
third floor piazza and his crest to
the parapet. The museum house is
operated by the Historic
Charleston Foundation.*

23 and 25 Meeting Street.

Here are variations on the single house theme. It's the detailing that makes the difference: color, roofline, "eyebrows" over the windows, and balconies.

25 Meeting Street.

Sea shapes — a fish fountain and earthquake bolts like starfish — grace this grotto-like entrance.

50

**Thomas Rose House,
59 Church Street.**

This house, built in 1735, did not get its piazza until the 20th century. When the gate is closed, the garden is an undisturbed retreat.

Ashley Hall, 172 Rutledge Avenue.

A girls' school since 1909, this Regency villa was built in 1816. Owners have included George A. Trenholm, Treasurer of the Confederacy, and the German consul, C. O. Witte, whose six beautiful and brilliant daughters, known as "the Witte girls," cast their aura over the social life of the city.

141, 143-145 Church Street.

These two tenements (the name only connotes rental property) were built in 1740 of "Bermuda Stone," a coral limestone underlying the island of that name. It's likely it was brought in empty ships as ballast.

Lamboll Street.

A lyre gate beckons.

53

**Philip Porcher House,
19 Archdale Street.**

*Philip Porcher's house, built
before the Revolution, was
within a block of the
disastrous 1861 fire. The
cypress he used just grows
more durable over the years
and needs no paint to
prevent rotting.*

Along South Battery.

Situated across from Battery Park, these houses all reach for their place in the sun — or their share of the breeze. The three on the right are from the 1850's and 60's and employ Italian design motifs. The house with the cupola, with its panoramic view of the harbor and lower city, dates from an earlier period.

Charleston, High Battery.

There have been various seawalls here since the 1750's, but most houses behind it date after 1820 when the area was made secure from the sea. The battery remains the most dramatic section of the city.

Charleston from the Harbor.

It's obvious why Josephine Pinckney called Charleston a "Sea-Drinking City."

57

2 Meeting Street.

Tradition has it that this splendid Queen Anne house was built by jeweler Waring P. Carrington for his bride in 1892. Her father built the Calhoun Mansion.

58

The Battery.

Monument to the Defenders of Fort Sumter.

White Point Garden and the Battery.

These "pleasure grounds" were laid out by 1850 when city council turned the seawall west at the edge of the city. Live oaks keep the park green throughout the year; cannon from various wars and a statue to Sgt. Jasper, hero of Ft. Moultrie, are among the monuments here. The two names come from history. The lower peninsula was often called White Point, and there were fortifications such as Broughton's Battery here by 1730.

The Sword Gates, 32 Legare Street.

These gates were commissioned by the city in 1838 for the Guard House, now the site of the Post Office. Christopher Werner made an extra pair, and a decade later, George A. Hopley acquired and added them to his house.

Garden, 57 Laurens Street.

Charleston was founded in April of 1670, and each succeeding spring, her gardens have rioted with color, as if celebrating.

38 and 40 Tradd Street.

Like most Charleston streets, Tradd takes its name from an early resident. Richard Tradd lived near here in the late 1670's. These two houses were built ca. 1718 and survived both the 1740 and 1778 fires. The unstuccoed brick building is the studio of Elizabeth O'Neill Verner.

23 Legare Street.

Reached by an alley and impossible to see from the street, this ca. 1838 house was the home of Charleston writer and naturalist Herbert Ravenel Sass who wrote of the birdwatching done in his secluded garden.

54 Tradd Street.

One of the older houses in the city, this one dates from 1740 and was the office and residence of Peter Bacot, appointed by Washington as postmaster. The balcony comes from another building.

Unitarian Church and St. John's Lutheran Church, Archdale Street.

Begun in 1772, it wasn't until 1787 that the Unitarian Church was finished. It was originally intended to serve the overflow of the Congregational Church on Meeting Street, but in 1839, the congregation changed its charter, becoming the first Unitarian church in the South. A long-time minister was Samuel Gilman, author of Harvard's anthem. The Lutheran minister John Bachman oversaw the construction of the church next door in 1818. The steeple, added later, is often considered to have been designed by the artist Charles Fraser. Bachman served the congregation until 1874, training the first black Lutheran ministers and writing the text for Audubon's Quadrupeds of North America. *Two of Bachman's daughters married Audubons. Following different ideas and doctrines, the congregations share a common mortality, meeting in their cemeteries.*

44 Charlotte Street.

Unlike other "shy" houses, the William Henry Houston house displays its porches proudly across its front. Nearby streets are named Elizabeth, John, Henrietta and Alexander, all after children of the Wragg family.

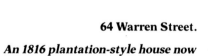

64 Warren Street.

An 1816 plantation-style house now completely surrounded by the city.

114 - 120, 122 East Bay.

Form has often evolved from function in the architecture of Charleston. Cupolas, such as the one on the Exchange Building, and lanterns, on Coates Row, give a glimpse of the harbor, telling merchants or customs officials when a ship is coming. The cupola on the Exchange Building is a modern replacement.

Laurens Street.

Piazzas, a pineapple post and palmettoes.

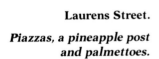

65

New Tabernacle Fourth Baptist Church,
22 Elizabeth Street.

Built for St. Luke's Episcopal Church, this building was consecrated in 1862 although it was not finished. Due to the Civil War, the church still remains steepleless. The ceiling rises 55 feet, and the gothic window is 37 feet high. The present congregation purchased the building in 1955. This is one of the highest areas in town — over 10 feet above sea level!

Magnolia Cemetery.

"The City of the Dead" opened north of the city about 1850.

Roper House, 9 East Battery.

With its Greek Revival portico and its balconies, the Roper House has an unparalleled view of the harbor just across the street. A 500-pound piece of cannon that fell through the roof in 1865 still rests in the attic.

67

Washington Park and the Ravenel House, 68 Broad Street.

Often known by its earlier name of "City Hall Park," this park was laid out about 1820 when the civic spirit of internal improvement seized Charleston. Its green lawn and oaks flank City Hall and the Fireproof Building on two sides. In its center rises a shaft built in memory of the Confederate dead, and in front of it is this statue of Henry Timrod, "the Poet Laureate of the Confederacy." There are other monuments on the arched wall, including one to Francis Salvador, first Jew to hold office in America and to die in the Revolutionary War. Behind the wall is the Ravenel House, built before 1800. It has always been owned and occupied by the same family.

Old Charleston Jail, 21 Magazine Street.

A fated place since its construction in 1802 and expansion in the 1850's, the jail has seen its share of villainy. Now awaiting fruitful use, it is unlike at least one of its inhabitants, who was much more certain of her destiny. Before she was hanged here for murder in 1820, Lavinia Fisher asked the crowds if anyone had a message for the Devil. She volunteered to take it.

74 Rutledge Avenue.

Like Charleston herself, this house keeps its secrets gracefully. Historians have been unable to pinpoint its construction, but it was probably built by 1800. There is no doubt at all about the garden. It's charming, offering itself up like a gift for any passerby caring to see.

15 Meeting Street.

John Edwards built this Georgian house by 1770; a decade later he was exiled by the British to St. Augustine. The family of Compte de Grasse (commander of the French fleet in the Revolution) refuged here after the Santo Domingan slave rebellion. The house is built of cypress with the boards on the facade scored to look like stone.

14 Legare Street.

Pineapples are a traditional symbol of hospitality. And that's what these gates are known as, although the finials are really more akin to the pinecones of classical Italy. George Edwards put them here and worked his initials in the wrought iron in 1816.

32 and 34 Montagu Street.

This row house, consisting of two units, was built in 1854 when the Italianate style was popular. A wall down the center divides even the piazzas.

31 Legare Street.

Earlier than most of its neighbors, this ca. 1789 house, built by rice planter Hannah Heyward, is distinguished by a rounded bay, a large garden and a ghost said to haunt the library. The tree branches in the foreground are crepe myrtle and will bear pinkish-red blossoms come summer.

20 Queen Street.

Once a cotton warehouse, this West-Indian style building, now a theatre, is the home of the Footlight Players.

42 Gadsden Street.

Even the outbuildings in Charleston are worthy of mention. This carriage house, now separate from the house it once served, was built about 1850.

73

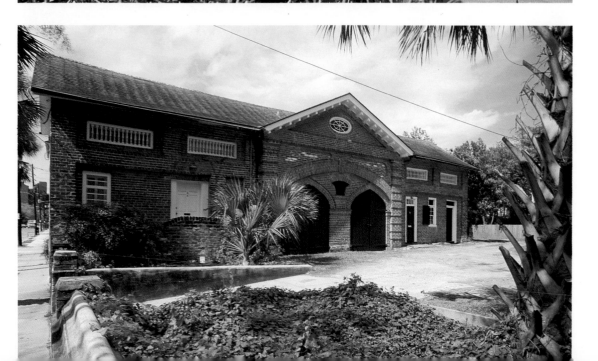

1 Tradd Street.

Colors in Charleston are often a collaboration. Man-chosen hues are worked and weathered by the moist sea air, and here, are mellowed further by the sunlight of early morning.

13 Pitt Street.

A cat may look upon a king, or he may stay home. It would be difficult to leave this garden.

74

Rainbow Row, East Bay Street, near Tradd.

It's easy to see why they call these buildings "Rainbow Row." They were built near the wharves that were once right across the street by merchants who lived upstairs and had offices below. The bright colors came with renovations in the 1920's and 30's.

34 Anson Street.

Piazzas, windows and transoms open up this town house to light, breezes and greenery. The house was built ca. 1848 when Philadelphia red brick, instead of the more common Carolina "grey," was enjoying a vogue in the city.

14 and 15 Thomas Street.

Two unusual buildings, an anachronism and a New England house, face each other across the corner of Warren and Thomas Streets. St. Mark's Episcopal Church was built a decade after the Civil War, after the Greek Revival phase had ended. Samuel S. Mills's house has many features reminiscent of his native Massachusetts.

Magnolia Gardens.

These informal gardens have been ranked with the Grand Canyon in natural beauty in early guide books to this country. Planted with azaleas and camellias and featuring romantic vistas and walkways, the gardens were begun ca. 1840 by John Grimke-Drayton. The house was moved here in 1873. Both are open to the public.

Middleton Place.

Only outbuildings, such as the spring house, and one wing, seen in the distance, were left standing after the Federal troops' 1865 visit. The gardens were more forgiving. Started in 1740, they are rekindled with color each season, and are the oldest landscaped gardens in the country. Terraced lawns, butterfly-shaped lakes, and a series of walkways and gardens, as well as the house, are open throughout the year.

Middleton Place Gardens.

Azaleas exult in the sunny, lush green setting.

78

Cypress Gardens.

Owned and kept open by the city, these gardens were made from the rice fields of Dean Hall Plantation. The cypresses rise to great heights, not branching until they reach the sun. Mysterious and stately, they also have knob-like roots called "knees" that project up from the water.

79

**Benjamin Dupre House,
317 East Bay Street.**

*Benjamin Dupre built his house
on the corner of George Street of
wood in 1803, using brick for a
more fireproof kitchen. The single
house to the right was moved to
this site to prevent its destruction
on another.*

80